ESKENAZI

ESKENAZI

**Chinese Buddhist sculpture
from Northern Wei to Ming**

18 March – 30 March 2002

**EXHIBITION
IN
NEW YORK
AT
PACEWILDENSTEIN
32 EAST 57TH ST
NEW YORK
NY 10022**
Telephone: 212-421 3237

Illustrated left
Contact sheet showing some of the cave
temple carvings at Longmen, Henan province.
(photography Giuseppe Eskenazi 1978)

**10 Clifford Street
London W1S 2LJ**
Telephone: 020 7493 5464
Fax: 020 7499 3136
e-mail: gallery@eskenazi.co.uk
web: www.eskenazi.co.uk

ISBN: 1 873609 12 4

Design Gordon House
Photography for all catalogue entries, except for no.12, Mike Bruce, London
Photography for catalogue no.12 Kerry Ryan McFate and Ellen Page Wilkinson, courtesy PaceWildenstein
Typeset Daniel M. Eskenazi, London, Kite Typesetters Ltd and Wordmill Graphics, London
Cartography p.12 Christopher Impey
Printed and originated by BAS, Hampshire

Foreword

This is our fifth exhibition entirely devoted to Chinese sculpture. Our first was held in 1978 and in the preface to that exhibition catalogue, I noted that it appeared to be the first to embrace the subject since 1944.

The situation has changed dramatically in the past twenty years: museums and other institutions, as well as dealers, have found an appreciative audience for a type of religious sculpture that is not necessarily instantly appealing nor particularly accessible. It can be both these things, however, as the now famous recent find of several thousand Buddhist stone figures and fragments at the Qingzhou temple site demonstrates. The sheer beauty of many of them has provoked universal admiration and some surprise, perhaps, that China – an ancient culture popularly associated with the highest achievement in almost every artistic sphere but that of three dimensional stone carving – can also compete honourably in this sphere. An exhibition of some thirty-five of the sculptures will reach the Royal Academy in London in April of this year, having visited the Altes Museum in Berlin and the Rietberg Museum in Zürich.

Our present exhibition, which this catalogue accompanies, is obviously far more modest in scope although I am very happy that we have been able to find examples (however fragmentary) from some of the most well-known cave temples of the Northern Wei – Tang period. We have also attempted to give a minute glimpse of the sheer range of Buddhist sculptural activity in China by including works in gilt bronze, wood and stucco as well as stone.

The exhibition will be held in New York, to coincide with Asia Week, at the PaceWildenstein gallery. I am extremely grateful to Arne Glimcher and to Richard Solomon of Pace Prints for accommodating us, once more, where we feel so much at home and for extending to us such warm and friendly assistance.

I would like to thank Edmund Capon, director of the Art Gallery of New South Wales, Sydney, and a foremost authority on Chinese sculpture and Buddhism, for finding the time – in an almost impossibly hectic schedule – to write the valuable and informative introduction to this catalogue.

I would also like to thank all in the gallery, particularly Sarah Wong and Yuansheng Wang, who have gone to great lengths to research and catalogue these sculptures – to most satisfactory effect.

Gordon House, as always, has been invaluable in the catalogue design and production and Mike Bruce has succeeded in photographing these works of art with fitting sensitivity.

Giuseppe Eskenazi

Fig. 1. Yungang cave temples, Shanxi province. Cave 20; seated Sakyamuni Buddha. Northern Wei, circa 460. *(photograph Joanna Capon)*

Fig. 2. Bingling cave temples, Gansu province. Cave 125; seated Sakyamuni and Prabhutaratna Buddhas. Northern Wei, early 6th century.

Metropolitan and Provincial - variations on themes in early Chinese Buddhist sculpture
By **Edmund Capon**

The great and inspiring images of China's major Buddhist cave temples, such as those at Yungang, Longmen, Maijishan and Gongxian, are the familiar and indelible icons of a great tradition. So definitive are they in their representation of the evolution of both style and content, and formidable in their physical presence, that they have become the hallmarks and the arbiters of the artistic character of early Buddhist art in China. The progress of artistic style is powerfully and convincingly demonstrated in these extraordinary rock-hewn monuments and yet, as recent revelations are demonstrating, regional variations of a dominant 'metropolitan' aesthetic did exist, just as they did in, for example, Shang and Zhou dynasty bronze ritual vessels.

Whilst it is inconceivable that any new finds could undermine the authority and presence of the imagery at these great cave temples, the excavations in recent years of groups of Buddhist sculptures from temple sites, often deliberately destroyed in the anti-Buddhist purges of the late Tang and Song dynasties, have shown the depth and potential for variations in artistic interpretation of the singular Buddhist style. It is true that at any one time a dominant stylistic idiom was widely and generally observed; the basic adherence to the classic mature late Northern Wei style in contemporary sculptures from distant Bingling si in Gansu and the Northern Liang sculptures from the Wanfo si and the more recently discovered (1995) works on Xian Road, both in Chengdu in Sichuan, demonstrate that widespread adherence to what might be described as a prevailing style.[1] However, other recent finds, in Sichuan, Hebei, Shandong, Shanxi, Ningxia and Gansu in particular have greatly enlarged our view of the perceived legacy of the classic 'metropolitan' style, for in these more outlying regions a local aesthetic has imposed a flavour of individuality and locality on Buddhist art.[2]

The most stunning of the recently excavated sites are those at Qingzhou in Shandong, but way back in 1954 the site of the Xiude si in Quyang, Hebei province, revealed a huge cache of over two thousand Wei to Tang marble Buddhist sculptures, mostly of small size. The marble figure of a Bodhisattva leaning against a tree, which almost certainly comes from an original group composed of a principal figure of a seated Maitreya (cat. no. 5), may well be associated with this group of sculptures, or with similar works from nearby temple sites in the area of Dingzhou, Hebei province.[3] The Quyang sculptures are seldom seen in any quantity and a large number remain in store in the Gugong in Beijing. Reflecting the mainstream stylistic evolution, these relatively modest but beautiful sculptures nonetheless form a remarkably homogeneous group and well illustrate the subtle imposition of a local aesthetic upon a pervasive and generally authoritative style. Interestingly another, much smaller group of marble sculptures discovered in 1997 near Shahe village, Huimin county, Shandong province with Eastern Wei and Northern Qi dates, assume a similar stylistic flavour to those of marble sculptures from Hebei, suggesting that it is not only locality but medium as well that has an impact upon artistic style.[4]

The same is true of the many finds from the two Qingzhou temples, the Longxing si and the Xingguo si, which date from the later Northern Wei to the Northern Qi periods.[5] Characterised by a refined and meticulous carving style, perhaps a consequence of the finely grained limestone, these Qingzhou sculptures adhere to the prevailing style but do so with their own distinctive aesthetic. It is one that is precise in its definition,

Fig. 3. Yungang cave temples, Shanxi province. Foyer to cave 10. Northern Wei, late 6th century. *(photograph Edmund Capon)*

Fig. 4. Large standing Sakyamuni Buddha; height 3.3m. Northern Zhou. Shanxi Provincial Museum, Taiyuan. *(photograph Edmund Capon)*

Fig. 5. Longmen cave temples, Henan province. Variocana Buddha and attendants, Fengxian si. Tang dynasty, 7th century. *(photograph Joanna Capon)*

urbane and often wonderfully simple in its concept and expression of volume and with a profound recognition of the balance between detail and simplicity. These sculptures fit perfectly into the pattern of stylistic evolution in that most distinguished era in the history of Chinese Buddhist sculpture, the sixth century, and yet they remain unquestionably distinctive and identifiable as a group. The head of a Northern Qi Bodhisattva in this exhibition (cat. no. 6) illustrates these definitive Qingzhou characteristics: firstly in the precision of the carving; secondly in the distinctive interpretation of the hairstyle, as such details seem to be a favoured idiom of the Qingzhou works; thirdly in the presence of substantial traces of gilt and, finally, in the refined consistency and colour of the limestone. Other sculptures from the Shahe village site, mentioned above, carved from the more familiar Shandong limestone also bear direct stylistic comparison with the Qingzhou works.

To a lesser degree local variations and stylistic idioms are apparent in cave temple carvings and sculptures. Here again the material – varying from the soft sandstone of Bingling si, to the grainy sandstone of Yungang, to the hard, dense grey limestone of the Longmen and Gongxian caves – has exerted considerable influence upon carving potential and thus to some extent style. The relative softness of the Yungang sandstone, for example, allows a certain fluency in these sculptures as illustrated in three works in the exhibition (cat. nos. 1,2,3), but does not permit the sharp definition achieved in the more meticulous Qingzhou carvings. The Yungang sculptures, therefore, differ noticeably in presence if not style, from those Northern Wei carvings at the Longmen and Gongxian temples which are but a decade or two later. The head of the meditating Bodhisattva from Yungang (cat. no. 1) is comparable with the heads in the panel from Gongxian (cat. no. 4) in terms of figurative interpretation, but the effect is quite different owing to the contrast between the soft sandstone of the former and the hard dense limestone of the latter. The impact that the type of stone has upon artistic style is further demonstrated in a comparison of the marble Quyang sculptures with the contemporary Qingzhou works: the former are almost sensuous in their subtle modelling, owing to the capacities of the stone, in contrast to the clarity and sharpness of the latter.

By the later sixth century when unified rule in China had dissipated, the support for Buddhism was far less assured and there was an even greater tendency to regional independence and interpretation. Under the sympathetic rule of the Northern Qi, Buddhism flourished in north and northeast China; the level of activity fostered local stylistic innovations, from Shanxi to Shandong, as the Qingzhou, Quyang and related sculptures testify. Under the roughly contemporaneous Northern Zhou in northwest China, however, Buddhism suffered purges and the destruction of Buddhist institutions; these actions were initiated by the Emperor Wu in 574 and extended over the rest of north China from 577, when the Northern Qi was conquered by the Northern Zhou. Such an atmosphere is reflected in artistic endeavour; for in place of the ravishing elegance of the Qingzhou sculptures and exquisite intimacy of the Quyang marbles of the Wei and Northern Qi periods, those Buddhist works made in Northern Zhou territory tend to be solid, unendearing monuments without spiritual sensitivity. It is a style perfectly illustrated in independent sculptures such as the somewhat immovable 3.3 metre high image of the Buddha in the Shanxi Provincial Museum in Taiyuan. Not surprisingly in such a political climate little work was undertaken at cave temples during the Northern Zhou rule. The more remote temples at Maijishan and Bingling si were probably the most active sites under Northern Zhou rule. Politics and locality thus conspired to create local stylistic diversions in Chinese Buddhist sculpture.

This regional diversity was less evident in the succeeding Sui and Tang dynasties, arguably because of political unity and strong imperial support. The work undertaken at the great imperially sponsored caves at Longmen is an enduring testament to a powerful liaison between church and state. Furthermore the sculptural style of those great cave temple works is the one that dominated in Tang Buddhist sculptural traditions, as evidenced in even quite intimate works such as the earthenware votive tablet (cat. no. 9) and more emphatically in the limestone group of Maitreya and attendants dated to 673 (cat. no. 11). There is an aesthetic consistency richly expressed in Tang Buddhist sculpture that extended to all corners of the empire, from Bingling si in Gansu, to individual sculptures from the Wanfo si in Chengdu in Sichuan, to the cave temples of Henan and Shandong provinces.

Notes

1. See *Wenwu*, 1998, volume 11, pages 4 - 20; and *Wenwu*, 2000, volume 2, pages 64 - 76.

2. Some of these are included in the exhibition *Monks and Merchants: Silk Road Treasures from Northwest China*, Asia Society, 2000. Of particular interest in the context of regional and provincial interpretations are catalogue nos. 56, 57, 58 and 59 which were found in Pengyang, Ningxia.

3. These and related finds are discussed in Li Jingjie and Tian Jun, 'Marble Buddhist images of the Dingzhou school', *Gugong Bowuguan Yuankan* (Palace Museum Journal), 1999, volume 3, pages 66 - 84.

4. *Wenwu*, 1996, volume 6, pages 70 - 81.

5. Sculptures from the Qingzhou sites have been included in a number of recent exhibitions, including the Museum of Chinese History, Beijing, 1999 and the Hong Kong Museum of Art, 2000.

Illustrated left
Fig. 6. Vairocana Buddha; Fengxian si, Longmen. Tang dynasty, 7th century. *(photograph Joanna Capon)*

Buddhist sites and temples

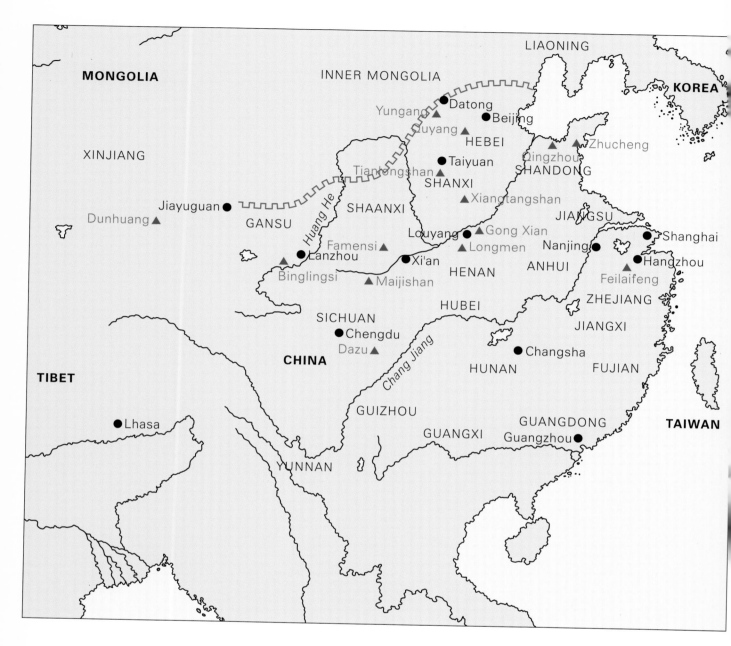

MONGOLIA

INNER MONGOLIA

LIAONING

KOREA

XINJIANG

Yungang ▲ ● Datong
Louyang ▲ ● Beijing

HEBEI

Zhucheng ▲

Tiantangshan ▲ ● Taiyuan

Qingzhou ▲

SHANDONG

SHANXI

Jiayuguan ●

SHAANXI

Xiangtangshan ▲

JIANGSU

Dunhuang ▲

GANSU

Huang He

Louyang ● ▲ Gong Xian

Famensi ▲

Longmen ▲

Nanjing ●

Shanghai ●

Lanzhou ●

Xi'an ●

Hangzhou ●

Binglingsi ▲

Maijishan ▲

HENAN

ANHUI

Feilaifeng ▲

ZHEJIANG

HUBEI

SICHUAN

Chang Jiang

JIANGXI

Chengdu ●

Dazu ▲

CHINA

Changsha ●

FUJIAN

TIBET

HUNAN

Lhasa ●

GUIZHOU

GUANGDONG

TAIWAN

GUANGXI

Guangzhou ●

YUNNAN

● Cities
▲ Sites or Temples
⊓⊔⊓⊔ Great Wall

Chronology
Chinese Dynasties and Periods
中国朝代

		BC 公元前	AD 公元
Xia period	夏	2100c – 1600c	
Period of Erlitou culture	二里头文化	1900 – 1600	
Shang period	商	1600c – 1027	
Zhengzhou phase	郑州阶段	1600 – 1400	
Anyang phase	安阳阶段	1300 – 1027	
Zhou period	周	1027 – 256	
Western Zhou	西周	1027 – 771	
Eastern Zhou	东周	770 – 256	
Spring and Autumn period	春秋	770 – 476	
Warring States period	战国	475 – 221	
Qin dynasty	秦	221 – 206	
Han dynasty	汉	206 –	220
Western Han	西汉	206 –	9
Xin dynasty (Wang Mang)	新（王莽）		9 – 23
Eastern Han	东汉		25 – 220
Six Dynasties period	六朝		220 – 581
Three Kingdoms	三国		220 – 280
Western Jin	西晋		265 – 317
Eastern Jin	东晋		317 – 420
Liu Song	刘宋		420 – 479
Southern Qi	南齐		479 – 502
Liang	梁		502 – 557
Chen	陈		557 – 589
Sixteen Kingdoms	十六国		304 – 439
Northern Wei	北魏		386 – 535
Western Wei	西魏		535 – 557
Eastern Wei	东魏		534 – 549
Northern Qi	北齐		550 – 577
Northern Zhou	北周		557 – 581
Sui dynasty	隋		581 – 618
Tang dynasty	唐		618 – 907
Five dynasties	五代		907 – 960
Liao dynasty	辽		907 – 1125
Song dynasty	宋		960 – 1279
Northern	北宋		960 – 1127
Southern	南宋		1128 – 1279
Jin dynasty	金		1115 – 1234
Yuan dynasty	元		1279 – 1368
Ming dynasty	明		1368 – 1644
Hongwu	洪武		1368 – 1398
Yongle	永乐		1403 – 1424
Xuande	宣德		1426 – 1435
Chenghua	成化		1465 – 1487
Hongzhi	弘治		1488 – 1505
Zhengde	正德		1506 – 1521
Jiajing	嘉靖		1522 – 1566
Longqing	隆庆		1567 – 1572
Wanli	万历		1573 – 1619
Tianqi	天启		1621 – 1627
Chongzheng	崇祯		1628 – 1644
Qing dynasty	清		1644 – 1912
Republic of China	中华民国		1912 – 1949
People's Republic of China	中华人民共和国		1949

Catalogue

**Chinese Buddhist sculpture
from Northern Wei to Ming**

1
Sandstone Bodhisattva
Northern Wei period, 386 - 535
Height: 42.0cm

Low relief sandstone carving of a Bodhisattva. The figure is shown in three-quarter view, seated in the 'pensive pose', with head slightly inclined to the right and cheek resting lightly on the fingers of the raised right hand. He is seated with the right leg crossed over the pendant left leg, and with the right ankle loosely clasped by the left hand. The Bodhisattva's elongated face has rounded cheeks, arched eyebrows, a broad nose and a small bud-like mouth. His head is crowned by a flaring, foliate tiara from which ribbons descend. The bare, upper torso is ornamented by a collared necklace, and a shawl is draped over the shoulders, falling in wide, shallow folds at the front. Traces of pigment are visible on the light grey sandstone.

Provenance:

An East Coast university museum collection, USA.

Both from the stylistic point of view and from the fact that it is sandstone, this figure may well come from the Yungang cave temples. See Seiichi Mizuno and Toshio Nagahiro, 'Yun-Kang: The Buddhist Cave-Temples of the Fifth Century A.D. in North China', volume 15, Kyoto, 1955, plate 86 for a view of Cave 39 showing several apparently similar meditating Bodhisattvas, generally placed in pairs on either side of a figure of Buddha.

The seated 'pensive figure' – with one leg crossed over the other and head resting on the hand – was a popular depiction in fifth and sixth century Chinese Buddhist sculpture. The figure is also found depicted independently and sometimes given the context of an arching *jambu* (roseapple) tree (or ginko tree). These pensive figures are generally identified as Maitreya – the Buddha of the Future – in the Tuṣita Heaven. Occasionally, it is clear from the surrounding narrative carvings that the figure is Siddhārtha[1] – when for instance one of the incidents from his life story is illustrated.

[1] Junghee Lee, 'The Origins and Development of the Pensive Bodhisattva Images of Asia', Artibus Asiae, volume 53: 3/4, Zürich, 1993, pages 311 - 357, where the author argues that the pensive figure in this position depicted in early Chinese Buddhist sculpture is usually Prince Siddhārtha.

一　思惟菩薩像　北魏　公元三八六年—五三五年

高四二・〇公分

沙岩质，浅浮雕。此像坐姿，头略右偏，右手托颊，右臂撑右腿上，右腿抬起搭于左膝，左腿垂放，左手松握右踝。菩萨面部略长，腮颊丰满，弯眉宽鼻，小嘴。头戴冠冕，缎带飘坠。袒胸带项圈饰，帔帛经肩而落，宽褶顺畅，沿小臂垂下。此像残存色斑依稀可见。

2
Sandstone Fragment from a figure of Buddha
Northern Wei period, late 5th century
Height: 35.0cm

Large buff sandstone fragment of the left hand of Buddha held in *vitarkamudrā*, resting lightly on the left knee. The well-rounded knee is covered by drapery delineated by a series of parallel bands that follow the curve of the thigh and fall vertically from the knee. The forearm is covered by the sleeve of the robe descending in thick vertical bands, stopping short of the wrist to reveal the fleshy hand. The grainy stone bears traces of blue and red pigments.

Provenance:

Yungang cave temples, Shanxi province, Cave 11, south wall, lower central part, niche 25a.

Private collection, Japan.

Exhibited:

Osaka, 1976, Osaka Municipal Museum of Art.

Izumi, 1984, Kuboso Memorial Museum.

Published:

Osaka Municipal Museum, 'Rikucho No Bijutsu', (Arts of the Six Dynasties), Tokyo, 1976, number 200.

Kuboso Memorial Museum, 'Chugoku No Bijutsu, Ichinin No Gan', (Chinese Art, One Man's View), Izumi, 1984, page 64, number 76.

See also:

Seiichi Mizuno and Toshio Nagahiro, 'Yun-Kang: The Buddhist Cave-Temples of the Fifth Century A.D. in North China', volume 8, Kyoto, 1953, plates 11, 12, 22 and 23a for the original location of this fragment.

The Buddha from which this fragment originates is positioned on the south wall of Cave 11, just above the entrance. The Buddha is shown seated in the 'European position', flanked by a standing Bodhisattva on each side. There are two niche sculptures in the cave, one on the east reveal of the window, and one on the east wall, with dated inscriptions, corresponding respectively to 495 and 483.

See catalogue number 3 for another fragment from a different cave at Yungang.

二

佛手及膝　北魏　公元五世纪晚期

高三五·〇公分

沙岩质。暗黄色残肢，仅存左手轻贴左膝，手施三宝印。膝头圆滚，宽条纹布褶，沿腿弯曲，顺膝下折。袖口齐腕，竖带纹饰。石面仍残留兰红色迹。

3
Sandstone Apsaras
Northern Wei period, late 5th century
Height: 37.4cm

Grey sandstone figure of a flying *apsaras* bearing an offering bowl. The *apsaras* floats as if reclining on the right elbow with a slender hand clasping the waistband, while the left arm raises the bowl. The head is shown in three-quarter view, with characteristic arched eyebrows, downcast eyes and broad nose. The small bud-like mouth is set in a sweet smile. The hair is drawn up to form a large, stiff, flaring topknot to which is attached a small section of the border which originally framed the piece. The *apsaras* wears a loose belted robe that falls open in a V-shape at the chest, and covers the extended legs in loose folds. Incised vertical bands at the front and rows of curved lines on the arms delineate the drapery. The grainy stone has a greyish-brown patina with traces of pigment.

Provenance:

Yungang cave temples, Shanxi province, Cave 1, south wall, east niche.

C.T. Loo, Paris and New York.

Bjorkman collection, Switzerland.

Published:

C.T. Loo and Co., 'An Exhibition of Chinese Stone Sculptures', New York, 1940, number 13, plate 8.

C.T. Loo and Co., 'Chinese Arts', New York, 1941 - 42, number 937.

See also:

Seiichi Mizuno and Toshio Nagahiro, 'Yun-Kang: The Buddhist Cave-Temples of the Fifth Century A.D. in North China', volume 1, Kyoto, 1952, plate 14, top right for what appears to be the original location of the *apsaras*.

The carving of the caves in the sandstone cliffs at Yungang began around 460, on the instructions of the Wei emperor Wencheng, in commemoration of the earlier Wei kings, and at the request of the Buddhist monk Tan Yao. Part of the reason was also to expiate the Buddhist persecutions of a few years earlier. Caves 1 and 2, together with Caves 5 and 6, which are stylistically linked, were finished by the early 480s. All four caves consist of a single chamber, entered through a narrow door and in each, there is an exuberantly carved central pillar. The walls and ceilings are covered with figures of all sizes, the largest figures often under canopies or set within architectural elements. The *apsarasas* are mainly confined to the ceilings and upper levels of the caves as befits their status as celestial beings.

See catalogue number 2 for another fragment from a different cave at Yungang.

三　飞天像　北魏　公元五世纪晚期

高三七·四公分

沙岩质。飞天左手持钵，飘逸潇洒。身倚右肘，右掌扣腰。头部微侧向钵，弯眉垂目宽鼻，小嘴含笑。髻鬟高耸，身穿长袍，开胸束腰，松褶盖腿，竖条纹勾勒出衣褶走向。此像表面有灰褐结层，并残留部分色痕。

四

礼佛图局部　北魏　公元六世纪前半期

长四三·七公分

花岗岩质。刻划了六名女性形象：最显著者是位贵妇，其体形大于他人，周围环境亦烘托出其身份。她右臂前伸展掌，左手持莲钵于腰。头部高浮雕，方脸微侧，弯眉尖额，口鼻适中。发束双鬟。五位侍女列次左右，均为椭圆脸，弯眉细目，嘴含笑意，温文而雅。头发髻式，单双各异。一女持钵腰际，其余袖手。所有皆着大袖开胸宽袍。此像上端有悬穗露出，应为主角的轮盖边饰。像间仍有红兰黄色痕遗留。

4

Limestone Panel

Northern Wei period, first half of the sixth century

Length: 43.7cm

Grey limestone panel, a fragment from a larger frieze, depicting a procession of six female figures. The most important figure in this group, probably an aristocratic lady, is depicted on a larger scale and with more space around her, indicating her significance. She stands with her right arm outstretched and palm flexed, while the left hand holds a lotus-shaped offering bowl to her waist. Her head is shown in three-quarter profile, and, like the other heads, is finely carved and in higher relief than the rest of the figure. Her square face, with arched eyebrows and well-defined nose and lips, terminates in a pointed chin. Her hair is neatly dressed in a double chignon. She is accompanied by five smaller figures, one to her left and four to her right, arranged in an overlapping row. Their oval faces are carved with arched eyebrows and downcast eyes, and their mouths set in a half-smiling, gentle expression. The attendants are differentiated by their hairstyles – some have double topknots, others have single buns. One of the figures holds a bowl to her waist, while another has her hands clasped inside her sleeves. All the figures wear loose robes, with full sleeves, and lapels forming a V-shape at the front and, in some cases, fastened with a wide band at the chest. Carved behind the figures are the handle of a fan, the upper part of which is missing, and a dangling tassel, probably from a parasol, which would have been held over the main figure. Traces of red, blue and yellowish pigments remain on the dark grey stone.

Provenance:

Gongxian cave temples, Henan province, Cave 1, south-west corner.

Hashimoto Kansetsu, Kyoto.

Exhibited:

Nagoya, no date, Aichi Prefectural Museum of Art.

Osaka, 1966, Osaka Municipal Museum of Art.

Osaka, 1976, Osaka Municipal Museum of Art.

Osaka, 1995, Osaka Municipal Museum of Art.

Published:

Aichi Prefectural Museum of Art, 'Toyo Bijutsu Bunka', (Oriental Art Culture), Nagoya, n.d., page 28, bottom right photograph.

Seiichi Mizuno, 'Chinese Stone Sculpture', Mayuyama and Co., Tokyo, 1950, plate 8, number 16.

Osaka Municipal Museum of Art, 'Chinese Stone Buddha Images', Kyoto, 1953, page 6, number 13.

M. Sato, 'Chugoku No Dogu', (Chinese Earthenware Figures), Tokyo, 1965, page 40, number 23.

Yuzo Sugimura and Burton Watson, 'Chinese Sculpture, Bronzes, and Jades in Japanese Collections', Tokyo and Honolulu, 1966, sculpture plates 12 - 13.

Osaka Municipal Museum of Art, 'Chugoku Bijutsu Gosen-nen Ten', (Exhibition of 5000 Years of Chinese Art), Osaka, 1966, page 8, figure 2-20.

Osaka Municipal Museum of Art, 'Rikucho No Bijutsu', (Arts of the Six Dynasties), Tokyo, 1976, number 215.

Osaka Municipal Museum of Art, 'Rikucho No Bijutsu', (Arts of the Six Dynasties), (Chinese Art Exhibition Series No. 2), Osaka, 1976, page 24, number 3-34.

Osaka Municipal Museum of Art, 'Chinese Buddhist Stone Sculpture: Veneration of the Sublime', Osaka, 1995, page 42, number 18.

See also:

'Gongxian shikusi', (Cave Sculptures of Gongxian), Beijing, 1963, pages 18 and 19, numbers 25 - 27 for the original location of the frieze.

Chen Mingda, ed., 'Zhongguo meishu quanji; diaosu bian 13: Gongxian, Tianlongshan, Xiangtangshan, Anyang shiku diaoke', (The Great Treasury of Chinese Art; Sculpture, volume 13: Gongxian, Tianlongshan, Xiangtangshan, Anyang – Cave Sculptures), Beijing, 1989, page 34, number 40 for what appears to be the original location with replacement figures.

Processions of devotees worshipping the Buddha became popular during the Northern Wei period, and are to be found at the Longmen and Gongxian cave temples amongst others. At Gongxian, Caves 1, 3 and 4 are decorated with friezes of devotees on the interior, flanking the entrance; the first two caves have three tiers of carvings on each side of the entrance, but Cave 4 has four incomplete tiers. Of all the Gongxian caves, the processional carvings in Cave 1 are apparently both the most complete and of the highest quality. The top and largest tiers represent the emperor (on the south-east wall) and the empress (on the south-western wall), each with entourage and attendants. Below the emperor are two panels representing male aristocrats and their attendants forming an impressive procession, while on the opposite side are the female aristocrats and their attendants, carved in two panels beneath the empress.[1] It would appear that the original location for the present fragment was at the back of the second tier, below the empress.[2]

Artistically these friezes display great virtuosity both in their sculptural and compositional qualities, employing high, low and medium relief carving to give a sense of perspective and depth. The second tier on the south-west wall of Cave 1 demonstrates this well. The whole panel is framed on either side by a tree, while a Buddhist nun leads at the front of the procession, holding an incense burner. The scene is further divided into 'cells' which move the eye along in a rhythmic way. There are four main figures, shown by their greater size, of which the larger figure in the present fragment is one; each is followed by four smaller attendants. The groups are separated in each case by a large canopy or umbrella over the main figure, and an oval fan behind her. It is possible that such friezes were based on paintings, now lost, as has been suggested in the case of some of the processional scenes at Longmen.[3]

It appears that the excavation at Gongxian started around 517, the second year when Lady Hu (consort to Emperor Xuanwu) assumed regency as Dowager Ling. She ruled as regent for her son from 515 - 520 and again from 525 - 528. It is probable that Caves 1 and 2 were built for Xuanwu (posthumously) and Lady Hu, and that the imperial donors carved on the south wall in Cave 1 are portrayals of them.[4] In addition, the friezes portray a cross-section of 6th century Chinese court society, all represented with a high degree of individuality.

[1] Chen Mingda, ed., 'Zhongguo meishu quanji; diaosu bian 13: Gongxian, Tianlongshan, Xiangtangshan, Anyang shiku diaoke', (The Great Treasury of Chinese Art; Sculpture, volume 13: Gongxian, Tianlongshan, Xiangtangshan, Anyang – Cave Sculptures), Beijing, 1989, pages 11, 12 and 13, and numbers 40 - 60. See also, T. Akiyama and S. Matsubara, 'Arts of China; Buddhist Cave Temples, new researches', Tokyo, 1969, page 231 for a line drawing of the southern wall in Cave 1.

[2] Osaka Municipal Museum of Art, 'Chinese Buddhist Stone Sculpture: Veneration of the Sublime', Osaka, 1995, page 42, number 18.

[3] Jan Van Alphen ed., 'The Buddha in the Dragon Gate', Antwerp, 2001, pages 76 - 78.

[4] See D. Wong, 'Women as Buddhist Art Patrons during the Northern and Southern Dynasties', in Wu Hung ed., 'Between Han and Tang: Religious Art and Archaeology in a Transformative Period', Beijing, 2000, page 545.

5
Marble Bodhisattva against a Tree-trunk
Northern Qi period, 550 - 577
Height: 37.5cm

White marble sculpture of a Bodhisattva standing on a foliate pedestal, carved in high relief in three-quarter view against the trunk of a tree. The deity presses his hands together in *añjalimudrā* against his bare chest, his head crowned with a diadem from which fall ribbons to either side and which fronts his tall topknot. He wears a shawl covering his shoulders and falling in loops to the front and a *dhotī* turned over at the waist to form a frill around the hips; a long, knotted sash hangs in front. There are traces of a painted necklace of beads remaining around his neck. The slightly curved trunk, with flat reverse left rough, is carved in places with whorling grain, as if indicating that branches had been cut from it. A rectangular tablet has been roughly incised over the Bodhisattva's head, on which was probably painted a name or title. The whole sculpture bears considerable traces of red and black pigments, with some stippled effects to imitate bark, and the surface is weathered all over except where chipped to reveal the micaceous white stone.

Provenance:

Private collection, Taibei.

Similar example:

Yang Boda, 'Quyang Xiudesi chutu jinian zaoxiang de yishu fengge yu tezheng', (The artistic style and features of dated small sculptures unearthed in Xiude temple in Quyang), Gugong bowuyuan yuankan, Beijing, 1960, volume 2, page 55, figure 27 for a fragmented Buddhist group in white marble showing a seated Buddha flanked by a pair of disciples standing against tree trunks, dated to the second year of Tiantong, corresponding to 566.

五 倚 树 菩 萨 像　北 齐　公 元 五 五 〇 年 ─ 五 七 七 年

五 倚 树 菩 萨 像

高 三 七 · 五 公 分

白 理 石 质 ， 高 浮 雕 。 菩 萨 足 踏 宝 台 ， 倚 树 而 立 ， 双 手 合 什 于 袒 胸 前 。 头 戴 冠 饰 ， 带 悬 两 侧 ， 发 系 高 髻 。 宝 缯 盖 肩 ， 垂 弯 胸 前 。 裙 袍 卷 起 饰 于 臀 部 ， 长 巾 前 挂 。 颈 间 遗 有 彩 绘 项 圈 痕 。 树 干 微 曲 ， 几 处 截 面 年 轮 清 晰 ， 菩 萨 上 部 有 长 方 形 空 白 处 ， 或 为 铭 录 。 通 体 有 红 黑 彩 迹 ， 风 化 的 表 面 有 斑 斑 云 母 质 白 石 显 露 。

6
Stone Head of a Bodhisattva
Northern Qi period, 550 - 577
Height: 26.0cm

Limestone head of a Bodhisattva crisply carved with arched brows and well-formed nose, above a delicate mouth and rounded chin. The elongated, half-closed eyes give the deity an expression of quiet contemplation. His hair is dressed in small comma-shaped curls, coiling to each side from the centre along the hairline to the front of the elongated ears. He wears an elaborate crown, centred by a lion mask with furrowed brow, with rosettes and flower-heads to the sides. The lion mask and the flower-heads – from which issue tassels – are enclosed within beaded borders. The reverse is left plain. The pale grey stone has an attractive smooth patina with traces of gilt.

Provenance:

C.T. Loo, Paris and New York.

Baroness Van der Elst, Brugge, Belgium.

Similar examples:

A. Salmony, 'Chinesische Plastik', Berlin, 1925, page 75, plate 59 for the head of a Bodhisattva wearing a crown with tassels, now in the University of Pennsylvania Museum of Archaeology and Anthropology. The same head is illustrated by O. Sirén, 'Chinese Sculpture from the Fifth to the Fourteenth Century', London, 1925, volume 4, plate 475c.

Wenwu, Beijing, 1991, volume 12, page 39, figures 6 and 7 for two Bodhisattva heads wearing crowns each decorated with a pearl roundel containing an animal mask, excavated from a Northern Qi pit at Xiyang, Shanxi province.

'Masterpieces of Buddhist Statuary from Qingzhou City', Beijing, 1999, page 130 for a Northern Qi Bodhisattva with a rosette with tassels in his headdress, and another on page 133 with a similar tasselled headdress.

It is not possible to identify the Bodhisattva exactly from the decoration on the headdress; it is, however, very much a product of its time, particularly the combination of beading and 'tassels'. The two similar examples cited immediately above from Qingzhou city, Shandong province, are among a group of very fine Northern Qi limestone standing and seated figures of Bodhisattvas with these crisply carved motifs in their headdresses. One of the two (on page 130) has remarkably similar curling hair to the head in the present exhibition. It appears likely that these motifs are, like Buddhism, not indigenous to China. Another rarer motif with Buddhist associations is the lion mask found on the present head and, as a pendant, as well as robe decoration, on one of the Qingzhou Bodhisattvas (page 133).

All these motifs – tassels, beads and lion masks – can also be found on 6th century ceramic vessels as applied decoration.[1]

[1] Suzanne G. Valenstein, 'Preliminary Findings on a 6th Century Earthenware Jar', Oriental Art, 1997/8, volume 43, number 4, pages 2 - 13.

六

菩薩頭像　北齊　公元五五〇年—五七七年

高二六·〇公分

石灰岩质。头像刻纹清晰，圆颏弯眉直鼻，唇形精细，眼线修长，双睑微睁，给人以瞑想深思的神情。卷浪纹发际，排列整齐，沿额前分至耳边。冠饰华丽，兽面居中，吞口喷珠，花团饰侧，珠穗琳琅。脑后素纹。石像表面光滑，金痕犹存。

七

佛三尊像碑

高六二·〇公分

北齐　公元五六三年

背屏式造像，石灰岩质。碑阳刻弥勒佛及胁侍菩萨，佛赤足立于莲台，双臂抬起，两手残缺（应施无畏与愿印）。佛面椭圆，小嘴弯眉，细目垂顾，顶上肉髻，波纹随形。帔帛复肩绕臂，宽褶U纹，流畅而下。内着僧祇支，系结胸前。两侧菩萨着袈裟，披巾横跨。头戴冠冕，下踏莲台，两鳞身螭龙曲颈盘体，口吐化莲，叶上小童嬉戏，莲荷上升化为圆台。佛脑后莲花头光，四外放射。背屏顶有浅浮雕螭龙，每侧伴一对飞天，手持火焰珠，飘逸而降。碑表面深色光滑，有红彩痕。碑阴刻有六十九字铭文。

7
Limestone Stele
Northern Qi period, dated 563 AD
Height: 62.0cm

Dark grey limestone stele of squared leaf-shape terminating in a stump at the base, carved with the figure of Maitreya Buddha, flanked by two Bodhisattvas. The Buddha stands upright upon a circular lotus pod base with arms raised and hands (now missing) probably once in *abhaya* and *varadamudrā*. His oval face is finely carved with a small mouth and arched eyebrows over the curved downcast eyes. The hair is arranged in wavy whorls over the prominent *uṣṇīsa*. He wears a shawl draped over the shoulders and arms, descending in U-shaped folds over the underskirt, and an undershirt fastened with a knotted bow. The Bodhisattvas are clad in loose-fitting monk's garments, with scarves crossing at the front, and on their heads are petal-form crowns with cascading ribbons on each side. Scaly, sinuous dragons, with undulating lotus stems issuing from their mouths, flank the Buddha. On one side the stems support a single chubby infant on a lotus flower, while on the other two infants frolic on a furled lotus leaf. In turn the infants support the circular bases on which the Bodhisattvas stand. Behind the Buddha's head a halo of incised petals radiates outwards, encircled by a band of short incised lines, a band of concentric circles and a band of scrolling lotus. The apex of the stele is carved in low relief with a descending dragon flanked on each side by a pair of *apsarasas* in flight. Each *apsaras* holds up a flaming pearl, as swathes of drapery and scarves flutter above. The smooth dark stone bears traces of red pigment. The reverse is incised with a 69 character inscription:

河清二年赵嗷鬼母成息康奴达阿兴念仁等丙寅清元年岁次
壬午池瓜朔清信士佛弟子等敬造弥勒像一躯上圣居家眷属
七世因缘遍地生生世世值佛出　　寺主僧归　僧乾

which can be translated as:

In the second year of the Heqing reign (corresponding to 563 AD), Zhao Dangui's mother passed away. Her children, Kang Nuda, Ar Xing (and) Nian Ren and others, all devoted Buddhists, reverently commissioned a stele of Maitreya in the early days of the autumn in the first year of Heqing (corresponding to 562 AD). May this bring salvation to the ancestors, all seven generations of the family, including the existing members, who worship devoutly.
The Temple Masters, Monk Gui, Monk Qian.

Provenance:

Private collection, Kyoto.

The cult of Maitreya was already very much in evidence by the sixth century in China, and is found, not only on free-standing sculpture, as in the present example, but also extensively depicted at the various Buddhist cave temples. Maitreya, as the Buddha of the Future, is known as the 'Compassionate One', and is the embodiment of universal love. According to the Buddhist scriptures, he is supposed to succeed Śākyamuni, the historical Buddha, as the Buddha of the coming age. Maitreya resides in the Tuṣita Heaven, where he preaches to *apsaras*as, and apparently will only appear when the teachings of Śākyamuni have been lost. Although Maitreya is in theory only a Bodhisattva, he is sometimes portrayed as a Buddha, as in the present example, befitting his future status.[1]

The small scale of the stele is unusual, incorporating as it does so many different elements such as *apsaras*as, the dragons, and in particular the small figures on lotuses at the feet of the Bodhisattvas – emblematic of the new souls being born in the Western Paradise of Amitābha, as described in the 'Sūtra on the Contemplations of Amitāyus'. In the sūtra, Queen Vaidehī appeals to Buddha who teaches her the practice of 'sixteen contemplations' so that she can reach the Pure Land where sorrow and misery no longer exist.[2]

[1] Dorothy C. Wong, 'Maitreya Buddha Statues at the University of Pennsylvania Museum', Orientations, February 2001, pages 24 - 31.

[2] Jan Van Alphen ed., 'The Buddha in the Dragon Gate', Antwerp, 2001, page 84.

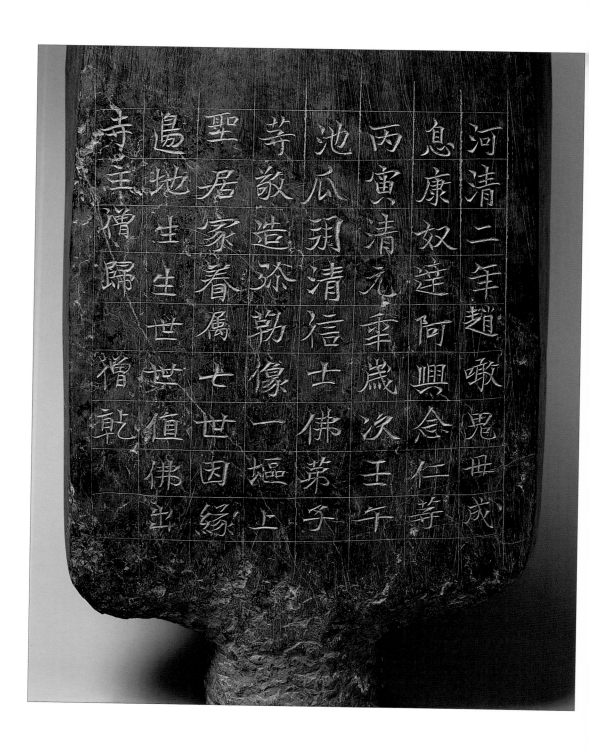

8
Marble Head of Buddha
Sui period, 581 - 618
Height: 22.0cm

Marble head of Buddha. The oval head is finely carved with a prominent *ūrṇā* between the high arching eyebrows which frame the partially closed, almond-shaped eyes. The well-defined nose is balanced by the delicate mouth, rounded chin and long well-formed ears. The hair, with bracket-shaped hairline, is arranged in rows of tight comma-shaped curls and covers the *uṣṇīsa* apart from a roundel of exposed flesh. The Buddha has an expression of meditative calmness. The white marble is partly covered with a dark reddish pigment which was perhaps the base for gilding, extensive areas of which still remain. There are traces of a brighter red colour, as well as blue and green pigments on the hair.

Provenance:

C.T. Loo, Paris.

Private collection, New York.

Published:

A. Salmony, 'Chinesische Plastik', Berlin, 1925, front cover and page 73, plate 58.

Similar example:

O. Sirén, 'Chinese Sculpture from the Fifth to the Fourteenth Century', volume 3, London, 1925, plate 328 for a complete figure with a similar head of comparable proportions.

It is unusual for a marble sculpture to retain such extensive areas of pigment and gilding. No doubt the face of the Buddha was originally completely covered by gilding, and the hair was a strong blue.

八　理石佛头像　隋　公元五八一年—六一八年

高二二·〇公分

此像刻艺精湛，椭圆头形，眉线突出，呈弯弧状，眉间白毫凸起。目形细长，眼睑微合，鼻正嘴小，双颊丰腴，两耳垂肩。低肉髻，螺旋发式，顶珠显露。原白理石为深红色所盖，间有绿色乳色，并残存贴金痕迹。

9
Earthenware Votive Tablet
Tang period, 7th - 8th century
Height: 21.5cm

Grey earthenware votive tablet of rectangular shape with a triangular apex decorated with a lion mask sporting pointed ears and fanged mouth; two *apsarasas* descend on the sloping sides with arms outstretched. The central shallow niche contains the figure of Buddha in high relief, seated in *dhyānāsana*, with right hand in *bhūmisparśamudrā* and left hand grasping his garment at the shoulder. His fine features are clearly discernible in the rounded face, topped by the smooth *uṣṇīsa*, and the whole head is framed by a large flame-shaped mandorla. The Buddha is clad in robes that fall in thick pleats down the front and over the arms. He is flanked by a pair of Bodhisattvas, each standing on a lotus pedestal, holding a lotus bud to the chest, the pendant arm and hand holding a heart-shaped attribute. On the outer columns, on either side of the Bodhisattvas, stand guardian figures, each in a menacing posture with legs apart and arms held to the chest with hands in balled fists. The lowest horizontal register, with narrow projecting edge, contains a single figure of a small child, representing the reborn soul, supported on chubby legs upon a lotus base with a muscular seated lion on either side of it. The reverse is plain with an area of roughness where it may once have been attached.

Provenance:

Alan Priest, New York.

Similar example:

'Hebeisheng Neiqiuxian Xingyao diaocha jianbao', (Neiqiu County: Investigation Report of Xing (Hsing)Yao Kiln in Neiqiu, Hebei), Wenwu, Beijing, 1987, volume 9, black and white plate 1, number 4 for an almost identical plaque (of a different ware) excavated from the Xing kilns in Neiqiu, Hebei province.

It appears that small-scale plaques such as this one were particularly popular from the early to mid Tang period. Referred to as *shanye foxiang*, they were apparently, in some instances, made by blending the ashes of deceased monks with clay, pressing the mixture into a mould and firing.[1] The plaques were then kept in temples or pagodas, probably for use by monks during personal devotions.

[1] Jia Maiming, 'Tang Chang'ancheng fosi yu Xi'an chutu de Tang nifoxiang', (Buddhist Temples of Tang Chang'an and the Excavated Tang Buddhist Votive Tablets from Xi'an), The National Palace Museum Monthly of Chinese Art, Taibei, September 1993, number 126, pages 72 - 81.

九　佛龕　唐　公元七世纪－八世纪

高二一·五公分

素烧陶瓷。龕为山形，角顶饰狮面纹，竖耳獠牙。两飞天沿斜边展臂飘落，高浮雕佛像居中，坐于束腰禅台，右手施降魔印，左手倚肩。佛面丰腴，肉髻发式，脑后背光。身着袈裟，落褶厚皱，盖至宝座。两侧有胁侍菩萨立于莲座上，一手持莲蕾于胸，另一手悬握心形宝器。最外侧各立一护法，双手握拳横胸，两腿叉开，姿式凶猛威武。底层中间有小儿形象，应为再生轮廻之意。两边各一蹲狮。龕背阴则滑糙参差。

10
Limestone Head of a Bodhisattva
Tang period, 618 - 907
Height: 36.0cm

Dark grey limestone head of a Bodhisattva, shown in three-quarter profile, rather than fully in the round. The whole figure was originally carved directly on to the wall of a cave to the proper left of a Buddha. The Bodhisattva has arched brows, elongated almond-shaped eyes and delicate full lips. The hair is braided, centrally parted and arranged into a tall topknot that is set in coils to either side and bound in front. The stone is covered in areas with remains of a gesso-like substance, the base for pigments, with traces of red surviving at the neck where broken off from the body.

Provenance:

Possibly from the Longmen cave temples, Henan province.

Private collection, France.

Private collection, England.

Genty collection, Spain.

Similar examples:

'Hai-Wai Yi-Chen: Chinese Art in Overseas Collections, Buddhist Sculpture II', Taibei, 1990, page 133, number 128 for a smaller head, formerly in the Heeramaneck collection and now in the Los Angeles County Museum; the same head was included in the exhibition 'The Arts of the T'ang Dynasty', Los Angeles, 1957, catalogue number 54.

O. Kümmel, 'Chinesische Kunst', (Exhibition of Chinese Art), Berlin, 1929, catalogue number 298.

The style of carving and the stone of which it is made suggest that this head may have originally come from one of the main Tang caves at Longmen, Henan province. The scale of the head indicates that the whole figure formed part of a trinity or a larger group of figures in which the Buddha was placed in the middle. An example of such a grouping is seen in the Jinan cave (built between 711 - 713).[1]

The Longmen cave temples were started shortly after 494, when the Northern Wei capital moved to Luoyang. As at Yungang some of the caves at Longmen, such as the Binyang cave, were under imperial patronage, but the many dedicatory inscriptions show that this was not invariably the case. Unlike at Yungang, where almost all the work was concentrated in a forty-year period before 500, the decoration of the caves at Longmen continued on a large scale until the end of the Tang period, to a greater or lesser degree of intensity. The head in the present exhibition is probably associated with the phase of decoration dating from the mid 7th to early 8th century, spanning the reigns of the Emperor Gaozong, the Empress Wu and her two short-lived successors. The most important caves and temples at Longmen created under the imperial patronage of Empress Wu include, amongst others, the Fengxiansi, the Dawanwufo Cave and the southern and northern Leigutai Caves.

[1] Wen Yucheng, ed., 'Zhongguo meishu quanji; diaosu bian 11: Longmen shiku diaoke', (The Great Treasury of Chinese Art; Sculpture, volume 11: Longmen Caves), Beijing, 1988, pages 168 - 171, numbers 171 - 174.

一〇 菩薩頭像 唐 公元六一八年—九〇七年

高三六・〇公分

深色石灰岩质。原像是直接雕刻于洞壁上，从脸朝的方向看，应为左胁侍菩萨。此像弧形眉式，长目微启，嘴唇丰满。发系辫式，曲卷向上呈高髻。像表面残留底料，颈部仍有红色遗痕。

11
Limestone Buddhist Group
Tang period, probably dated to 673
Height: 57.1cm

Grey limestone group comprising Maitreya Buddha flanked by Ananda on the right, and Kaśyapa on the left, and a pair of Bodhisattvas, set within an arched niche. The figure of Buddha is seated in *dhyānāsana* on a draped, waisted throne supported on a lotus petal base, with one hand in *bhūmisparśamudrā* and the other, now missing, probably once in *abhayamudrā*. The Buddha's robes fall in folds between his legs and a shawl is draped over the shoulders above the half-bare torso. His face is full, with pronounced features and arching brows, and his hair is arranged in large tight spirals over a rounded *uṣṇīsa*. Ananda and Kaśyapa are clad in monk's robes and stand with feet slightly apart on circular waisted pedestals, and hands clasped at the chest. Ananda is characterized by a smooth shaven head and fine features, while Kaśyapa is distinguished by his furrowed brow, drawn features and defined neck muscles. The flanking Bodhisattvas stand, slightly swaying, on circular pedestals, each with one hand at the side entwined with a scarf that drapes over the shoulders. The other hand is flexed, in one case at the chest, and in the other, raised to the shoulder, probably once holding attributes. Both wear necklaces and sashes across the bare torsos, and skirts that fall in deep folds to the ankles. The hair of each Bodhisattva is arranged in a topknot. The head of each figure is encircled by a circular or leaf-shaped mandorla. The reverse of the niche is left plain. The thick base is carved on one corner with a kneeling female donor figure presenting an offering; the opposite corner is now partially missing. The base is incised with a 59 character dedicatory inscription, a few characters of which appear to have been recarved:

佛弟子王智文妻张清信为敬造阿弥陀像一铺上为皇帝皇后

先祖父母合家大小常德安乐法界苍生解脱忧苦俱登正觉

咸熙（？）四年九廿二日造成

which can be translated as:

The Buddhist disciples Wang Zhiwen and his wife Zhang Qingxin respectfully commissioned an image of Maitreya, for (the salvation) of the emperor, the empress, and all the ancestors, parents and family members, wishing them happiness, peace, and all release from suffering, (as well as) all good fortune.
Made in the fourth year of Xianxi(?), on the twenty-second day of the ninth (month).

一一　佛龕　唐　公元六七三年

高五七・一公分

石灰岩质。拱形龛含五尊像：佛像居中，结跏趺坐于高莲台上，手施无畏与愿印。迦叶阿难分列左右，两侧各一菩萨。佛袍垂褶腿间，帔帛落肩，前胸半袒。佛面圆满，五官清晰，螺纹肉髻。两弟子身穿袈裟，双手合什，面容各俱特色。两胁侍菩萨帔帛过肩，一臂下垂，另一胸前，手持宝器，均袒胸带项圈，裙袍褶顺至踝。发呈高髻。四人均

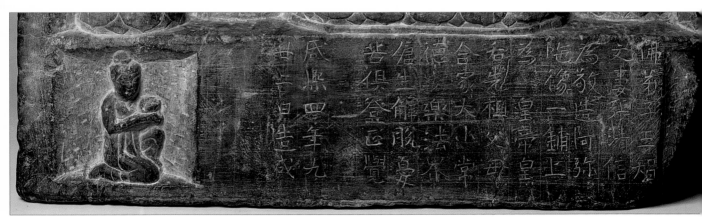

C. W. Matthes, Queeckhoven, Holland.

Similar examples:

Jin Shen, 'Zhongguo lidai jinian foxiang tudian', (Illustrated Chronological Dictionary of Chinese Buddhist Figures), Beijing, 1994, page 346, number 261 for a very similar example in the Rietberg Museum dated to the third year of Xianheng (corresponding to 672).

Saburo Matsubara, 'A History of Chinese Buddhist Sculpture', volume 3, Tokyo, 1995, plate 690b for a niche sculpture with pointed arch dated to the seventeenth year of Kaiyuan (corresponding to 729); also Osaka Municipal Museum of Art, 'Zui To No Bijutsu', (Arts of the Sui and Tang Dynasties), Tokyo, 1978, number 293.

A. Salmony, 'Chinese Sculpture', exhibition at the M.H. de Young Memorial Museum, San Francisco, 1944, plate 22, for a similar Tang period niche sculpture with donor, inscribed with an apocryphal Northern Wei date.

One of the recarved characters on the present sculpture is the second part of the reign title which now reads Xianxi. There was no such reign title in the Tang period but there were two reign titles starting with Xian: Xianheng (corresponding to 670 - 673) and Xiantong (corresponding to 860 - 873). Almost certainly, the present sculpture should be dated to the fourth year of Xianheng (673), as it is so strikingly similar to the example in the Rietberg Museum with its inscription dating it to 672.

The cult of Maitreya was popularized during the 7th and early 8th centuries, partly as a result of the influence of the Empress Wu. As the consort of Gaozong (r.649 - 683), she was enthroned as the empress in 655. She wielded tremendous influence over imperial and state affairs and by 660, when Gaozong apparently suffered a stroke, she effectively ruled the empire, in fact, if not in name, until 690, when she founded her own Zhou dynasty (690 - 705). The text of a minor sūtra called *Mahāmegha* or *Tayun* (Great Cloud) was used by her supporters to reinforce her claim to legitimacy as it contained a prophecy of 'the imminent reincarnation of Maitreya as a female deity, monarch of all the world'[1]. One of her acts of patronage was to found state-maintained Great Cloud Temples in every prefecture of the empire, and she later incorporated the words 'Maitreya the Peerless' into her title.

[1] Ed. Denis Twitchett and John K. Fairbank, 'The Cambridge History of China: Sui and T'ang China, 589 - 960, Part I', volume 3, Cambridge, 1979, pages 305 - 306.

立于束腰圆台上。五尊像皆有背光。龛背素面。龛底一角刻跪姿女供养人，相对处残缺。中间刻有五十九字铭文。

12
Limestone Hand
Late Tang period, 9th - 10th century
Height: 36.0cm

Large limestone hand of a Buddha or a Bodhisattva. The right hand is raised with rounded palm turned outwards, the first and middle fingers held upright and the thumb and fourth finger touching, possibly in a variant of *vitarkamudrā*. The hand is modelled fully in the round, the plump fingers with curved nails and creases at the joints, the life line finely incised on the palm. The stone is of dark tone, with some weathering.

Provenance:

Walter Weinberger, London.

David Part, Wiltshire.

Private collection, New York.

Similar examples:

Alan Priest, 'Chinese Sculpture in the Metropolitan Museum of Art', New York, 1944, catalogue number 44, plate 86, for a hand of Buddha from the Longmen cave temples.

Wen Yucheng, ed., 'Zhongguo meishu quanji; diaosu bian 11: Longmen shiku diaoke', (The Great Treasury of Chinese Art; Sculpture, volume 11: Longmen Caves), Beijing, 1988, page 107, number 110, for a large Buddha with similar raised right hand in situ at the north cave at Binyang, Longmen.

一二 佛手 唐晚期 公元九世纪—十世纪

高三六·〇公分

石灰岩质。此乃右手（或佛或菩萨），形态硕大，手掌抬起，掌心向外。食指中指合拢伸直向上，拇指内合，会及无名指，施三宝印。此手肥厚饱满，指甲皱纹及掌中脉络清晰。石表面因风化而泛黑。

13
Gilt Bronze Bodhisattva Avalokiteśvara

Tang period, early 8th century
Height (from pedestal): 26.0cm

Gilt bronze figure of Avalokiteśvara, probably originally eleven-headed, standing in *tribhaṇga* on a circular pedestal. The deity wears a *dhotī* falling to the ankles in deeply cast U-shaped folds, swathed around the hips and knotted below the stomach, and a sash draped across the chest over a necklace. The main head is surmounted by the four remaining smaller heads, in the form of a diadem from which hang plaits of hair and sashes, now partly missing. The back of the head is set with a tenon for the attachment of a mandorla. The figure is richly gilt with some areas of dark patina.

Provenance:

Otto Burchard, Berlin.

Oscar Gerson, Berkeley.

Elizabeth Kavaler, San Francisco.

Reach collection, Geneva.

Exhibited:

London, 1978, Eskenazi (on loan from the Reach Family Collection).

London, 1989, Eskenazi.

Published:

Eskenazi, 'Ancient Chinese Sculpture', London, 1978, number 6.

Eskenazi, 'Chinese Art from the Reach Family collection', London, 1989, number 3.

Saburo Matsubara, 'A History of Chinese Buddhist Sculpture', volume 3, Tokyo, 1995, plates 765a and b.

Similar examples:

Toshio Nagahiro, 'Toyo Bijutsu Choso', (Asiatic Art in Japanese Collections – Sculpture), volume 3, Tokyo, 1968, plate 60; also Li Yumin, 'Zhongguo jitongfo', (Chinese Buddhist Gilt Bronzes), The National Palace Museum Monthly of Chinese Art, Taibei, March 1988, number 60, page 88, bottom left.

Osaka Municipal Museum of Art, 'Zui To No Bijutsu', (Arts of the Sui and Tang Dynasties), Tokyo, 1978, plate 307.

For a detailed study of the eleven-headed Avalokiteśvara, see, S.E. Lee and W.K. Ho, 'A Colossal Eleven-faced Kuan-Yin of the T'ang Dynasty', Artibus Asiae, volume 22: 1/2, Ascona, 1959, pages 121 - 137.

一三 菩萨立像 唐 公元八世纪早期

通高二六·〇公分

铜铸鎏金。原应有十一个头，立于圆形宝台上，裙袍贴身下垂，深褶至踝，宽带绕臀，系于腹部，披帛斜跨胸前璎珞。顶部仍有四颗小佛头，列成花冠形置于辫发之上。头后部有突出的榫子，用于安装背光。此像鎏金厚实，杂以部分锈痕。

14
Gilt Bronze Bodhisattva
Yuan period, 1279 - 1368
Height: 28.0cm

Gilt bronze Bodhisattva seated in the position of royal ease, *lalitásana*, cast with the left leg pendant and foot resting on a spiky double-petalled lotus, and right knee up, with foot placed on a textured mat. The right arm rests on the right knee, while the slender fingers of the left hand are placed lightly on the trailing scarf; each wrist is encircled by a bracelet. His plump oval face is sweetly expressive with the small mouth set in a faint smile. The arched eyebrows which lead to the narrow bridge of the aquiline nose frame the downcast, heavy-lidded eyes. The neatly coiffed hair is secured above the forehead with a diadem and parts at the back into two tresses, each falling in three curling strands down the shoulder. The Bodhisattva wears an elaborate necklace descending in two double loops down the bare torso while bud-shaped tassels emerge from a central rosette. The underskirt is finely incised with a border of floral scrolls and falls in folds down the lower leg. A knee-length overskirt, edged with a narrow band of flower-heads, is pulled up high on the small of the back, and falls open at the front; another short garment is folded over the studded belt falling in folds between the legs. The shoulders are draped with a wide shawl which is threaded through the arms and curves to the feet where it terminates in flame-like points. The gilding has an attractive reddish-gold tone with extensive traces of red pigment.

Provenance:

John Sparks Ltd, London.

Private collection, London.

Similar examples:

Sherman E. Lee and Wai-Kam Ho, 'Chinese Art Under the Mongols: The Yüan Dynasty (1279 - 1368)', Cleveland, 1968, catalogue number 9, for the 14th century gilt bronze Guanyin in the British Museum.

René-Yvon Lefebvre d'Argencé, 'Chinese, Korean and Japanese Sculpture in The Avery Brundage Collection', Tokyo, 1974, plate 154 for a gilt bronze Guanyin dated to the 14th century.

William Watson, 'L'Art de la Chine', Paris, 1997, page 415, number 472 for a smaller figure dated to the Song dynasty, in the Ashmolean Museum, Oxford; also, Daisy Lion-Goldschmidt, 'Chinese Art: Bronze, Jade, Sculpture, Ceramics', London, 1960, page 280, number 126.

These gilt bronze Bodhisattvas in the pose of 'royal ease' (presumably originally resting on a rockwork base in gilt bronze, or in another material) are generally referred to as the 'Water and Moon' (Shuiye) Guanyin, or the 'Southern Seas' (Nanhai) Guanyin, seated as if on the rocky shore of Mount Potalaka.

一四　菩薩坐像　元　公元一二七九年─一三六八年

高二八·〇公分

铜铸鎏金。菩萨半跏趺坐，左腿自然下垂，足踏莲台，右腿抬起，右手搭膝，左手扶帛，手腕均带镯。面相雍容端祥，嘴含笑意，弯眉直鼻，眼睑饱满，目光下视。头发梳理整齐，束冠以饰，后垂两辫，沿肩顺落，项圈精美，璎珞琳琅。内袍边沿花纹细刻，褶纹流畅及脚。外袍饰花带边，另一短衫自束腰垂皱褶于腿间。宽帔贴肩绕臂卷曲而落，莲花纹刻饰其上，两端呈火焰纹状。此像鎏金泛红，几处有红彩，但整体显得富丽辉煌。

15

15
Gilt Bronze Buddha
Ming dynasty, Zhengde period, with a cyclical date corresponding to 1506
Height: 61.5cm

Gilt bronze figure of Amitābha Buddha standing upright with feet apart and hands in *abhaya* and *varadamudrā*. His broad face, which radiates a feeling of calm, is set with downcast eyes, a wide nose and a small bud-like mouth. His dark hair is arranged in neat curls over the top of the head and the prominent *uṣṇīsa*. A *kāṣāya* is worn diagonally across his body, over the left arm and shoulder and partially draped on his right shoulder, falling in deep U-shaped folds down the front. The underskirts flare out beneath in two undulating layers. All are decorated with an incised border of scrolling lotus. The figure stands on a separate oval-shaped lotus base with a double row of petals and a central flowerhead cast with 'seeds'. The figure is covered, apart from the hair, with gold leaf on a red lacquer ground. A twelve-character inscription is incised on the inner sleeve of the figure:

丙寅年榮府造阿弥陀佛一尊

which can be translated as:

In the *Bingyin* year a figure of the Amitābha Buddha was commissioned by the Rong household.

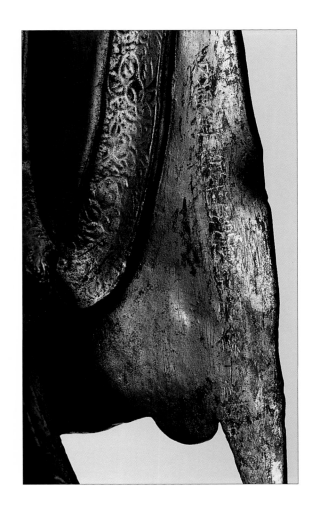

一五　佛立像　明正德　公元一五〇六年

高六一・五公分

銅鑄鎏金。阿弥陀佛立于蓮花座上，雙腳分開，手施無畏與願印，面部丰滿，神色安祥，垂目寬鼻，小嘴丰唇。深色發螺紋肉髻，頂珠于上。袈裟斜披，蓋左肩臂，部分搭于右肩，U型衣紋垂于前。內袍下露兩層波紋褶皺，呈喇叭狀，並飾以蓮紋邊。像背無飾。蓮花座為雙層橢圓形。此像金箔復蓋，紅漆為地。佛袍袖內刻十二字銘文。

Provenance:

Ralph M. Chait, New York.

Mayuyama and Co., Tokyo.

Mr and Mrs René Rivkin collection, Sydney.

Exhibited:

Tokyo, 1973.

Published:

Hugo Munsterberg, 'Sculpture of the Orient', New York, 1972, plate 107.

Mayuyama and Co., 'Chugoku ko toji masahin shoten ten kan toroku', (Illustrated Catalogue of a Small Exhibition of Masterworks of Ancient Chinese Ceramics), Tokyo, 1973, page 20, number 20.

Jin Shen, 'Zhongguo lidai jinian foxiang tudian', (Illustrated Chronological Dictionary of Chinese Buddhist Figures), Beijing, 1994, page 418, number 322.

Similar example:

W. Zwalf, 'Buddhism: Art and Faith', London, 1985, number 302 for the smaller figure of Amitābha, dated 3rd year of Chenghua (corresponding to 1467) in the British Museum; also, Hugo Munsterberg, 'Chinese Buddhist Bronzes', Rutland, Vermont and Tokyo, 1967, plate 31 for another image of the same figure; see also, 'Hai-wai Yi-chen: Chinese Art in Overseas Collections; Buddhist Sculptures', Taibei, 1986, number 168.

There were five *Bingyin* years during the Ming dynasty with dates corresponding to 1386, 1446, 1506, 1566 and 1626. 'Rong' is the contraction of a title conferred five times during the Ming period. The only individual who held the 'Rong' title during a *Bingyin* year was Zhu Youshu, the thirteenth son of the Chenghua emperor, also known as Rongzhuang wang. He was given his title in 1491, and died in 1539, as recorded in the Ming histories.[1] 'Rong fu' must therefore refer to the household of this person.

[1] Zhang Tingyu ed., 'Ming shi', (History of the Ming Dynasty), volume 104, page 1966, and volume 119, page 2410, Beijing, 1736, reprinted, Beijing, 1999.

16
Wood Bodhisattva
Jin - Yuan period, 12th - 13th century
Height: 142.0cm

Carved hollow wood figure of a Bodhisattva standing on a pedestal, with left arm down and missing right forearm once raised. The figure has a full face with slightly parted fleshy lips, black eyes and long hair parted and swept up into a topknot that is fronted by a diadem carved with a lotus base and jewelled buckle; bound tresses of hair, some missing, fall gracefully over the shoulders. The belted tunic worn by the Bodhisattva is held up by one studded strap with fringed end – so leaving the chest mostly bare – and falls in pleats over the thighs to an irregular hem; under this the *dhotī* is gathered at the calves, the material drawn up to reveal the extant bare right foot. The wide belt has rope-twist borders and is set with carved rectangular plaques, partly hidden in front by a pendant sash with loosely knotted bow. A collared shawl, with pleats and folds, covers the shoulders and back and an elaborate necklace, carved with dragon fish confronting a roundel with pendant bud, hangs at the chest. The surface of the wood is still partly covered by gesso bearing traces of gilding and painted in a few areas with remnants of green, red and black pigments.

Provenance:

Paul Houo-Ming-Tse, Paris.

Gérard Devillers, Paris.

Published:

Paul Houo-Ming-Tse, 'Preuves des Antiquités de Chine', Beijing, 1930, page 314, left hand side.

Hôtel Drouot, 'Objets d'art de la Chine: Collection Paul Houo-Ming-Tse', Paris, 1932, number 84.

Similar examples:

O. Sirén, 'Kinas Konst Under Tre Årtusenden', volume 2, Stockholm, 1943, figure 122 for a standing Bodhisattva, now in the Royal Ontario Museum, Toronto.

'L'Illustrazione Italiana: Testimonianze d'arte orientale', year 1, number 3, Milan, Autumn, 1974, plate 18 for a Bodhisattva of very similar proportions in the National Museum of Oriental Art, Rome.

Large wood sculptures were made in the north in Shanxi province to adorn temples; they were often made of the local catalpa wood (*tong*) and were invariably painted and gilded. They occasionally survive with dated tablets such as the large famous Guanyin (height: 190.5cm) from the modern Linfen prefecture in southern Shanxi, and now in the Royal Ontario Museum, dated 1195[1], and a Guanyin in the Metropolitan Museum, New York, dated 1282.[2] However, it seems likely that the tradition of carving these large wooden figures dates from an earlier period.

[1] Barbara Stephen et al., 'Homage to Heaven, Homage to Earth: Chinese Treasures of the Royal Ontario Museum', Toronto, 1992, plate 104.

[2] Alan Priest, 'Chinese Sculpture in the Metropolitan Museum of Art', New York, 1944, plate 116.

一六　观音立像　金元　公元十二世纪—十三世纪

高一四二・〇公分

木雕像。观音立于宝台上，左臂下垂，右臂抬起（小臂残缺）。面容丰满，五官清晰，长发分缕向上成高髻，饰以宝冠，冠上刻有莲台及珠宝扣。长辫紧束，沿肩自然顺落。外袍系腰，褶纹流畅至腿，袒胸跣足。绞式宽腰带，长方扣饰，部分被垂缨遮住。帔帛复盖肩背，胸前项圈精美。像表面仍部分残留底料，并有贴金色及绿红黑色迹。

一七　共命鳥像　明　公元一三六八年—一六四四年

高三二‧三公分

夾紵漆，鐵架芯。像為人面鳥形，臀部右偏。雙首塑造精細：面容飽滿，圓鼻彎眉秀目，緞帶飄自腦後，並飾花冠。前胸寬實，羽翼豐滿。帔帛繞肩，下着及膝葉片片裙，系以寬帶于腰。雙手作揖，鳥腿修長，兩爪立于貼金雲座上。像正面貼金，並着綠色于裙，兰色于發。

17
Stucco Figure of a Deity
Ming period, 1368 - 1644
Height: 32.3cm

Stucco figure of a double-headed deity modelled on an iron armature standing with hips swaying to the right. Each of the plump faces has delicately formed features with rounded nose, and chin, with painted arched eyebrows over the curved eyes. Fluttering ribbons issue from the back of the heads, each of which is encircled by a simple diadem. The broad chest supports both fleshy necks, and a pair of finely feathered triangular wings emerges from the back. A wide shawl is draped around the shoulders and the figure wears a leaf skirt, fastened with a wide belt, falling in undulating strands to the knees. The arms are held in front of the chest with hands respectfully clasped and the slender, gnarled bird-like legs terminate in elongated claws resting on a tuft of gilded cloud. The front of the figure is covered with gilding, with green pigment on the skirt and blue pigment on the hair.

Provenance:

Alan Priest, New York.

Similar examples:

'Buddhist Sculpture of Shanxi Province', Beijing, 1991, for various identical stucco figures included amongst the temple ornaments in Xiaoxitian Temple, Xi county: plate 19, middle column, second row from the bottom for a very similar figure; plate 31, right hand column, second row from the bottom for another view of the figure; plate 57 behind the Buddha on the right, for another double-headed figure; plate 63, left hand column, second row from the bottom; plate 263 for two figures flanking the main figure of Buddha.

Mary Shepherd Slusser, 'Nepalese Unfired Clay Sculpture: A Case Study', in Orientations, September 2001, page 78, figure 6, for the Chinese winged double-headed figure from the Singer collection, now in the Arthur M. Sackler Gallery, Smithsonian Institution, Washington D.C.

The figure in the present exhibition appears to be based on the Buddhist legend of the *gongming* or *mingming niao* (the bird of shared destiny) – a bird with two human heads, each head possessing a distinct personality.[1] One day, one of the heads noticed, while the other was sleeping, a luscious flower which it decided to consume without waking the other. When the sleeping one awoke, it was furious at being left out and vowed to revenge itself. It waited until the other was asleep and ate a poisonous flower that killed them both. The original moral of the story is now unclear – it may have been intended to point out that a Jekyll and Hyde exists in all of us, or it may have been illustrating the perils of a relationship based on jealousy. However, as a popular decorative motif it survived in various media, including metalwork and temple furnishings.[2]

[1] Wenwu cankao ziliao, Beijing, 1956, number 4, front cover and page 28 for an account of this legend. See also, William Edward Soothill and Lewis Hodous, 'A Dictionary of Chinese Buddhist Terms', London, 1937, reprinted Delhi, 1977, page 336.

[2] Li Mingzhong, 'Shiyin Song Li Mingzhong yingzao fashi', (Architectural Methods), volume 33, originally published 1103, reprinted Nanjing, 1919, page 9, for a line drawing of a *gongming niao* included in a group of architectural designs and patterns.

See also catalogue numbers 18 and 19.

18
Pair of Stucco Bodhisattvas
Ming period, 1368 - 1644
Height: 33.8cm and 36.0cm

Pair of stucco figures of Bodhisattvas modelled on iron armatures, each facing front with hips thrust forward, rounded shoulders and head tilted downwards. The figures are in complementary positions, standing with one hand raised and the other lowered. Each has a plump face set with downcast eyes, broad nose and delicate mouth. The hair on each figure is neatly dressed in a topknot and encircled by a diadem decorated with rosettes. Each Bodhisattva wears a garment falling in V-shaped folds over the underskirt, extending over one arm and round the shoulders, leaving the chest bare. The front of the figures is covered with gilding and traces of red pigment, and the hair is coloured with blue pigment.

Provenance:

Alan Priest, New York.

Similar examples:

'Buddhist Sculpture of Shanxi Province', Beijing, 1991, plate 31, for similar stucco figures included amongst the temple ornaments on the pillars in Xiaoxitian Temple, Xi county.

Eskenazi, 'Ancient Chinese Sculpture from the Alsdorf Collection and others', London, 1990, numbers 21 and 22, for two stucco figures of an earlier date.

The Xiaoxitian Temple and various temples in Shanxi are profusely decorated with wood and stucco sculpture which have been particularly well preserved, partly due to climate conditions in the area. The temples range in date from the Liao period through to the late Qing period, and due to the fragile nature of the material were subject to renovation from time to time.

See also catalogue numbers 17 and 19.

一八 菩薩像一對 明 公元一三六八年─一六四四年

高三三·八公分 三六·〇公分

夹纻漆，铁架芯。菩萨立姿，腹部微挺，肩部丰圆，俯首垂面。两尊像呈相对姿势，手式一起一落。菩萨圆脸，目光俯视，口鼻适度。发束高髻，环以花冠。身穿长袍，前胸袒露。衣纹披落，复盖内袍。像正面贴金，红迹残留。头发则着兰色。

19
Pair of Stucco Bodhisattvas
Ming period, 1368 - 1644
Height: 34.0cm and 34.4cm

Pair of stucco figures of Bodhisattvas modelled on iron armatures, each standing with one shoulder thrust forward, and arms extended across the waist, in mirror image of each other. The figures have plump faces with pointed chins and small, fine features; the hair is dressed in a topknot and encircled by a diadem. Each Bodhisattva wears a long underskirt falling in flat folds to the bare feet, over which is fastened an overskirt that falls in sharp folds from the belted waist; a shawl is arranged over the shoulders. The front of the figures is covered with gilding, with traces of red pigment, and the hair is coloured with blue pigment.

Provenance:

Alan Priest, New York.

Similar examples:

'Buddhist Sculpture of Shanxi Province', Beijing, 1991, plate 31, for similar stucco figures included amongst the temple ornaments on the pillars in Xiaoxitian Temple, Xi county.

Eskenazi, 'Ancient Chinese Sculpture from the Alsdorf Collection and others', London, 1990, numbers 21 and 22, for two stucco figures of an earlier date.

See catalogue numbers 17 and 18.

一九　菩薩像一對　明　公元一三六八年——一六四四年

高三四・〇公分　三四・四公分

夾紵漆，鐵架芯。菩薩立姿，一肩前趨，臂於腰際，兩尊姿勢相對。菩薩面容豐滿，下頜微收，眉目清秀，髮系高髻，環以冠飾。身著長內袍，皺折垂落跣足，外袍束腰，下褶井然。帔帛蓋肩。像均正面貼金，紅迹殘留，頭髮則著兰色。

Bibliography

Aichi Prefectural Museum of Art, *Toyo Bijutsu Bunka, (Oriental Art Culture)*, Nagoya, n.d.

Akiyama, T. and Matsubara, S.: *Arts of China; Buddhist Caves Temples, new researches,* Tokyo, 1969.

Archives of the Chinese Art Society of America/Archives of Asian Art, New York, 1945-.

Ars Orientalis, Washington DC, 1954-.

Artibus Asiae, Dresden, Ascona and Zürich, 1925-.

Arts of Asia, Hong Kong, 1978-.

Ashton, L.: *An Introduction to the Study of Chinese Sculpture*, London, 1924.

Buddhist Sculpture of Shanxi Province, Beijing, 1991.

Bulletin of the Museum of Far Eastern Antiquities, (BMFEA), Stockholm, 1929-.

Capon, E.: *Art and Archaeology in China*, Sydney, 1977.

Capon, E.: *Tang China, Vision and Splendour of a Golden Age,* London, 1989.

Chen Mingda ed., *Zhongguo meishu quanji; diaosu bian 13: Gongxian, Tianlongshan, Xiangtangshan, Anyang shiku diaoke,* (The Great Treasury of Chinese Art: Sculpture, volume 13: Gongxian, Tianlongshan, Xiangtangshan, Anyang - Cave Sculptures), Beijing, 1989.

Ch'en, K.: *Buddhism in China*, Princeton, 1964.

d'Argencé, R-Y.L. et al.: *Chinese, Korean and Japanese Sculpture in the Avery Brundage Collection*, Tokyo, 1974.

Davidson, J.L.: *The Lotus Sutra in Chinese Art*, New Haven, 1954.

Dubosc, J-P. et al.: *Chinese Art*, Venice, 1954.

Eskenazi, *Ancient Chinese Bronze Vessels, Gilt Bronzes and Sculpture: two private collections, one formerly part of the Minkenhof Collection*, London, 1977.

Eskenazi, *Ancient Chinese Sculpture*, London, 1978.

Eskenazi, *Ancient Chinese Sculpture*, London, 1981.

Eskenazi, *Chinese Art from the Reach Family collection*, London, 1989.

Eskenazi, *Ancient Chinese Sculpture from the Alsdorf Collection and others*, London, 1990.

Eskenazi, *Sculpture and ornament in early Chinese art,* London, 1996.

Eskenazi, *Chinese Buddhist Sculpture,* London, 1997.

Fogg Art Museum, *Grenville L. Winthrop: Retrospective for a Collector*, Cambridge, Massachusetts, 1969.

Goepper, R. et al.: *Meisterwerke aus China, Korea und Japan*, Cologne, 1977.

Gongxian shikushi, (Cave Sculptures of Gongxian), Beijing, 1963.

Gugong bowuyuan yuankan, (The Palace Museum Journal), periodical, Beijing, 1958-.

Hai-Wai Yi-Chen, Chinese Art in Overseas Collections: Buddhist Sculptures, Taibei, 1986.

Hai-Wai Yi-Chen, Chinese Art in Overseas Collections: Buddhist Sculpture II, Taibei, 1990.

Henan Sheng Bowuguan, (Henan Provincial Museum), wenwu press, Beijing, 1985.

Hôtel Drouot, *Objets d'art de la Chine: Collection Paul Houo-Ming-Tse*, Paris, 1932.

Houo-Ming-Tse, P.: *Preuves des Antiquitiés de Chine*, Beijing, 1930.

Howard, A.F.: *Chinese Buddhist Sculpture from the Wei through the Tang Dynasties*, Taibei, 1983.

Huang Wenkun and Liu Xiaodai: *Zhongguo wenwu jinghua*, (Gems of China's Cultural Relics), Beijing, 1992.

L'Illustrazione Italiana: Testimonianze d'arte orientale, Milan, 1974.

Jenkins, D.: *Masterworks in Wood: China and Japan*, Portland Art Museum and Asia House Gallery, New York, Portland, 1976.

Jin Shen: *Zhongguo lidai jinian foxiang tudian*, (Illustrated Chronological Dictionary of Chinese Buddhist Figures), Beijing, 1994.

Kaogu (Archaeology), Monthly periodical, Beijing, 1956-.

Kaogu xuebao (Archaeologia Sinica), Quarterly periodical, Beijing, 1954-.

Kaogu yu wenwu (Archaeology and Cultural Relics), Periodical, Xi'an, 1980-.

Kümmel, O.: *Chinesische Kunst*, Exhibition, Berlin, 1929.

Lawton, T. et al.: *Asian Art in the Arthur M. Sackler Gallery: The Inaugural Gift,* Washington DC, 1987.

Lee, S.E. and Wai-Kam Ho: *Chinese Art Under the Mongols: The Yuan Dynasty (1279-1368)*, Cleveland, 1968.

Li Jingjie: *Shifo xuancui*, (Essence of Buddhistic Statues), Beijing, 1995.

Li Mingzhong: *Shiyin Song Li Mingzhong yingzao fashi*, (Architectural Methods), volume 33, originally published 1103, reprinted Nanjing, 1919.

Liaoning Sheng Bowuguan, (Liaoning Provincial Museum), wenwu press, Beijing, 1983.

Lin Shuzhong, ed.: *Zhongguo meishu quanji, diaosu bian 3, Wei Jin Nanbeichao diaosu*, (The Great Treasury of Chinese Art, Sculpture volume 3, Wei, Jin and Six Dynasties Sculpture), Beijing, 1988.

Lion-Goldschmidt, D. and Moreau-Gobard, J-C.: *Chinese Art: Bronze, Jade, Sculpture, Ceramics*, London, 1960.

Liu Xiaodai, ed.: *Quanguo chutu wenwu zhenpin xuan*, (A Selection of the Treasure of Archaeological Finds of the People's Republic of China), Beijing, 1987.

Loewe, M.: *Ways to Paradise, The Chinese Quest for Immortality,* London, 1979.

Loo, C.T.: *An Exhibition of Chinese Stone Sculptures*, New York, 1940.

Loo, C.T.: *Chinese Arts*, New York, 1941 - 42.

Ma Yue et al.: *Xi'an - Legacies of Ancient Chinese Civilization*, Beijing, 1992.

Masterpieces of Buddhist Statuary from Qinghzhou City, Beijing,1999.

Matsubara, S.: *A History of Chinese Buddhist Sculpture*, 4 volumes, Tokyo, 1995.

Mayuyama and Co., *Chugoku ko toji masahin shoten ten kan toroku*, (Illustrated Catalogue of a Small Exhibition of Masterworks of Ancient Chinese Ceramics), Tokyo, 1973.

Menzies, J: *Buddha: Radiant Awakening,* Sydney, 2001.

Miho Museum, *Longmen Caves*, catalogue, Shigaraki, 2001.

Mizuno, S.: *Chinese Stone Sculpture*, Mayuyama and Co., Tokyo, 1950.

Mizuno, S.: *Bronze and Stone Sculpture of China*, Tokyo, 1960.

Mizuno, S. and Nagahiro, T.: *Yun-Kang: The Buddhist Cave-Temples of the Fifth Century A.D. in North China*, 20 volumes, Kyoto, 1952.

Munsterberg, H.: *Chinese Buddhist Bronzes*, Rutland, Vermont and Tokyo, 1967.

Munsterberg, H.: *Sculpture of the Orient,* New York,1972.

Nagahiro, T.: *Toyo Bijutsu Choso*, (Asiatic Art in Japanese Collections – Sculpture), volume 3, Tokyo, 1968.

The National Palace Museum of Chinese Art, monthy periodical,Taibei, 1983-.

Nickel, L.: *Die Rückkehr des Buddha*, (travelling exhibition to Altes Museum, Berlin, Museum Rietberg, Zürich and Royal Academy of Arts, London), Zürich, 2001.

Oriental Art, Quarterly periodical, London, 1948-.

Oriental Ceramic Society, Transactions, London, 1923-.

Orientations, Hong Kong, 1981-.

Osaka Municipal Museum of Art, *Chinese Buddhist Stone Sculpture: Veneration of the Sublime*, Osaka, 1995.

Osaka Municipal Museum of Art, *Chinese Stone Buddha Images,* Kyoto, 1953.

Osaka Municipal Museum of Art, *Chugoku Bijutsu Gosen-nen Ten*, (Exhibition of 5000 Years of Chinese Art), Osaka, 1966.

Osaka Municipal Museum of Art, *Rikucho no Bijutsu*, (Arts of the Six Dynasties),Tokyo, 1976.

Osaka Municipal Museum of Art, *Rikucho no Bijutsu*, (Arts of the Six Dynasties),(Chinese Art Exhibition Series No. 2), Osaka, 1976.

Osaka Municipal Museum of Art, *Zui To No Bijutsu*, (Arts of the Sui and Tang Dynasties), Tokyo, 1978.

Ostasiatische Zeitschrift, periodical, Berlin, 1912 - 1942.

Priest, A.: *Chinese Sculpture in the Metropolitan Museum of Art*, New York, 1944.

Qin Tingyu: *Zhongguo gudai taosu yishu,* (The Art of Ancient Chinese Ceramic Sculpture), Beijing, 1957.

Revue des Arts Asiatiques, Museum periodical, Paris, 1924-.

Royal Academy of Art, *International Exhibition of Chinese Art*, London, 1935.

Salles, G.: *Arts de la Chine Ancienne*, Paris, 1937.

Salmony, A.: *Chinesische Plastik*, Berlin, 1925.

Salmony, A.: *Chinese Sculpture*, Exhibition at the M.H. de Young Memorial Museum, San Francisco, 1944.

Sato, M.: *Chugoku No Dogu*, (Chinese Earthenware Figures), Tokyo, 1965.

Schafer, E.H.: *The Golden Peaches of Samarkand*, Berkeley, 1963.

Shi Yan, ed.: *Zhongguo diaosu shi tulu*, (Illustrated History of Chinese Sculpture), 4 volumes, Shanghai, 1983 - 1990.

Shi Yan, ed.: *Zhongguo meishu quanji diaosu, bian 4, Sui Tang diaosu,* (The Great Treasury of Chinese Art, Sculpture volume 4, Sui and Tang Sculpture), Beijing, 1988.

Shi Yan, ed.: *Zhongguo meishu quanji, diaosu bian 5, Wudai Song diaosu*, (The Great Treasury of Chinese Art, Sculpture volume 5, Five Dynasties and Song Sculpture), Beijing, 1988.

Sirén, O.: *Chinese Sculpture from the Fifth to the Fourteenth Century*, 4 volumes, London, 1925.

Sirén, O.: *Kinas Konst under Tre Årtusenden*, Stockholm, 1942.

Sirén, O.: *Chinese Sculptures in the von der Heydt Collection*, Rietberg Museum, Zürich, 1959.

Soothill, W. E. and Hodous, L.: *A Dictionary of Chinese Buddhist Terms*, London, 1937, reprinted Delhi, 1977.

Stephen, B. et al: *Homage to Heaven, Homage to Earth: Chinese Treasures of the Royal Ontario Museum*, Toronto, 1992.

Sugimura, Y. and Watson, B.: *Chinese Sculpture, Bronzes and Jades in Japanese Collections*, Tokyo and Honolulu, 1966.

Trubner, H.: *The Arts of the T'ang Dynasty*, Los Angeles County Museum, 1957.

Twitchett, D. and Fairbank, J.K.: *The Cambridge History of China: Sui and T'ang China, 589 - 960, Part I*, volume 3, Cambridge, 1979.

Van Alphen, J. ed.: *The Buddha in the Dragon Gate*, Antwerp, 2001.

Visser, H.F.E.: *Asiatic Art*, Amsterdam, 1948.

Wang Ziyun: *Zhongguo diaosu yishu shi, 1 & 2,* (History of Chinese Sculpture, volumes 1 & 2), Beijing, 1988.

Watson W.: *L'Art de la Chine*, Paris, 1997.

Weidner, M. ed.: *Latter Days of The Law: Images of Chinese Buddhism 850 - 1850*, Kansas, 1994.

Wen Yucheng, ed.: *Zhongguo meishu quanji; diaosu bian 11: Longmen shiku diaoke*, (The Great Treasury of Chinese Art: Sculpture, volume 11: Longmen Caves), Beijing, 1988.

Wenwu (Cultural Relics), Monthly periodical, Beijing, 1955-.

Wenwu cankao ziliao, Monthly periodical , Beijing, 1950-.

Wu Hung ed.: *Between Han and Tang: Religious Art and Archaeology in a Transformative Period*, Beijing, 2000.

Zeng Zhushao et al.: *Ancient Chinese Buddhist Sculpture: The C.K. Chan Collection*, Taibei, 1989.

Zhang Tingyu ed.: *Ming shi*, (History of the Ming Dynasty), volume 104 and 119, Beijing, 1736, reprinted, Bejing, 1999.

Zwalf, W. ed.: *Buddhism: Art and Faith*, The British Museum, London, 1985.

Works of art purchased from the Eskenazi Galleries, London, are now in the following museum collections:

Ackland Art Museum, North Carolina

Arita Porcelain Park Museum, Saga

Art Gallery of New South Wales, Sydney

Art Gallery of South Australia, Adelaide

Art Institute of Chicago, Chicago

Arthur M. Sackler Gallery, Washington, DC

Arthur M. Sackler Gallery, Boston

Art Museum, Princeton University, Princeton

Ashmolean Museum, Oxford

Asia House, Mr and Mrs John D Rockefeller 3rd Collection, New York

Asian Art Museum of San Francisco, San Francisco

Asian Civilisations Museum, Singapore

Baltimore Museum of Art, Baltimore

Birmingham Museum of Art, Alabama

British Museum, London

Brooklyn Museum, New York

Chang Foundation, Taibei

Cincinnati Art Museum, Cincinnati

Cleveland Museum of Art, Cleveland

Columbus Museum of Art, Columbus

Corning Museum of Glass, Corning

Dallas Museum of Fine Arts, Dallas

Denver Art Museum, Denver

Didrichsen Art Museum, Helsinki

Fitzwilliam Museum, Cambridge

Flagstaff House Museum of Teaware, Hong Kong

Freer Gallery of Art, Washington, DC

Fuji Art Museum, Tokyo

Hagi Uragami Museum, Hagi

Hakone Museum of Art, Hakone

Hetjens Museum, Düsseldorf

Hong Kong Museum of Art, Hong Kong

Honolulu Academy of Arts, Honolulu

Idemitsu Museum of Arts, Tokyo

Indianapolis Museum of Art, Indianapolis

Israel Museum, Jerusalem

Istituto Italiano per il Medio ed Estremo Oriente, Rome

Kimbell Art Museum, Fort Worth

Kuboso Memorial Museum, Izumi City, Osaka

Los Angeles County Museum, Los Angeles

Matsuoka Museum of Art, Tokyo

Metropolitan Museum of Art, New York

Miho Museum, Shigaraki

Minneapolis Institute of Arts, Minneapolis

MOA Museum of Art, Atami

Musée Ariana, Geneva

Musée des Arts Asiatiques, Nice

Musée Guimet, Paris

Musées Royaux d'Art et d'Histoire, Brussels

Museum für Kunst und Gewerbe, Hamburg

Museum für Lackkunst, Münster

Museum für Ostasiatische Kunst, Berlin

Museum für Ostasiatische Kunst, Cologne

Museum of Decorative Art, Copenhagen

Museum of Fine Arts, Boston

Museum of Fine Arts, Houston

Museum of Oriental Ceramics, Osaka

Museum Rietberg, Zurich

National Gallery of Australia, Canberra

National Gallery of Canada, Ottawa

National Gallery of Victoria, Melbourne

National Museum, Singapore

National Museum, Tokyo

Nelson-Atkins Museum of Art, Kansas City

Norton Simon Museum of Art at Pasadena, Pasadena

Östasiatiska Museet, Stockholm

Royal Ontario Museum, Toronto

St. Louis Art Museum, St. Louis

Seattle Art Museum, Seattle

Shanghai Museum, Shanghai

Speed Art Museum, Louisville

Toguri Museum of Art, Tokyo

Tsui Museum of Art, Hong Kong

Victoria & Albert Museum, London

Virginia Museum of Fine Arts, Richmond

Previous Exhibitions

March 1972	Inaugural exhibition Early Chinese ceramics and works of art.
June 1973	Ancient Chinese bronze vessels, gilt bronzes and early ceramics.
November 1973	Chinese ceramics from the Cottle collection.
December 1973	Japanese netsuke formerly in the collection of Dr Robert L Greene.
June 1974	Early Chinese ceramics and works of art.
November 1974	Japanese inrō from the collection of E A Wrangham.
May 1975	Japanese netsuke and inrō from private collections.
June 1975	Ancient Chinese bronzes from the Stoclet and Wessén collections.
June 1976	Chinese jades from a private collection.
June 1976	Michael Birch netsuke and sculpture.
June 1976	Japanese netsuke and inrō from private collections.
June 1977	Ancient Chinese bronze vessels, gilt bronzes and sculptures; two private collections, one formerly part of the Minkenhof collection.
June 1978	Ancient Chinese sculpture.
June 1978	Michael Webb netsuke.
June 1978	Eighteenth to twentieth century netsuke.
June 1979	Japanese netsuke from private collections.
June 1980	Japanese netsuke from private collections and Michael Webb netsuke.
July 1980	Ancient Chinese bronzes and gilt bronzes from the Wessén and other collections.
December 1980	Chinese works of art from the collection of J M A J Dawson.
October 1981	Japanese netsuke and inrō from the collection of Professor and Mrs John Hull Grundy and other private collections.
December 1981	Ancient Chinese sculpture.
October 1982	Japanese inrō from private collections.
October 1983	Michael Webb, an English carver of netsuke.
October 1984	Japanese netsuke, ojime, inrō and lacquer-ware.
June 1985	Ancient Chinese bronze vessels, gilt bronzes, inlaid bronzes, silver, jades, ceramics – Twenty five years.
December 1986	Japanese netsuke, ojime, inrō and lacquer-ware.
June 1987	Tang.
June 1989	Chinese and Korean art from the collections of Dr Franco Vannotti, Hans Popper and others.
November 1989	Japanese lacquer-ware from the Verbrugge collection.
December 1989	Chinese art from the Reach family collection.
May 1990	Japanese netsuke from the Lazarnick collection.
June 1990	Ancient Chinese sculpture from the Alsdorf collection and others.
November 1990	The Charles A Greenfield collection of Japanese lacquer.
June 1991	Inlaid bronze and related material from pre-Tang China.
November 1992	Japanese lacquer-ware – recent acquisitions.
December 1992	Chinese lacquer from the Jean-Pierre Dubosc collection and others.
June 1993	Early Chinese art from tombs and temples.
June 1993	Japanese netsuke from the Carré collection.
June 1994	Yuan and early Ming blue and white porcelain.
June 1995	Early Chinese art: 8th century BC-9th century AD.
October 1995	Adornment for Eternity, loan exhibition from the Denver Art Museum.
June 1996	Sculpture and ornament in early Chinese art.
November 1996	Japanese inrō and lacquer-ware from a private Swedish collection.
March 1997	Ceramic sculpture from Han and Tang China.
June 1997	Chinese Buddhist sculpture.
June 1997	Japanese netsuke, ojime and inrō from the Dawson collection.
November 1997	Japanese netsuke – recent acquisitions.
March 1998	Animals and animal designs in Chinese art.
June 1998	Japanese netsuke, ojime and inrō from a private European collection.
November 1998	Chinese works of art and furniture.
March 1999	Ancient Chinese bronzes and ceramics.
November 1999	Ancient Chinese bronzes from an English private collection.
March 2000	Masterpieces from ancient China.
November 2000	Chinese furniture of the 17th and 18th centuries.
March 2001	Tang ceramic sculpture.
November 2001	Tang ceramic vessels 500 – 1000 AD.